ABOUT THE AUTHOR

Dr. Mary Alice Jones is one of this country's recognized authorities on religious education for children and is the author of many best-selling children's books in the field of religion. She had prepared this book especially to help parents with their important task of bringing little children to know of God's love.

GOD LOVES ME

By Mary Alice Jones

Illustrated by Elizabeth Webbe

R AND M^cN ALLY & C OMPANY · CHICAGO
Established 1856

How do I know God loves me?
Let me think of the ways.

I think of my mother and daddy.
They love me
    and take care of me.

God planned

for mothers and daddies.

That's how I know God loves me.

I smell the flowers in my yard,

I see their colors,

    red, gold and blue,

I touch the petals so very soft.

God planned the flowers
   I like so much.
That's how I know God loves me.

I taste the apples from my tree,
I eat my cereal
and carrots crisp.

God plans good food
for me to eat.
That's how I know God loves me.

With my feet, I run and dance,

With my hands,

    I build with blocks,

  Zip the zippers on my clothes,

Paint a picture with my brush.

I am strong and steady, too,
Pull my wagon, ride my bike.

God planned my body
so I could move
And use my hands
and grow up strong.

That's how I know God loves me.
I like the day when it is light,
And I can see to work and
     play;

I like the night when it is dark

And I can snuggle down to sleep

While the moon sails

   through the clouds.

God plans for day,
  God plans for night.
That's how I know God loves me.

When the wind blows hard
   and the thunder is loud,
And the lightning flashes
   in the sky,
I close my eyes and think of God.

God speaks in my heart,
    "Be not afraid."
That's how I know God loves me.

I like my church
   with the big wide door,
And the people
   who come there to pray.

The big people come
and the children come
And my minister is there
to meet them.
God plans for me
to have a church.
That's how I know God loves me.

I touch the Bible
    my teacher holds
And listen as she reads to me:
"God loves you.
    He cares about you."

God plans for me
   to have the Bible.
That's how I know God loves me.

My mother tells me of Jesus
Who loved all the children
And showed them the way
To love one another.
God plans for me to know Jesus.
That's how I know God loves me.

How do I know God loves me?
I think of all the ways.

Then I close my eyes and say,
"Thank you, God, for loving me."